the GIFT *of the* HAWK

the GIFT of the HAWK

randy lundy

COTEAU BOOKS
WWW.COTEAUBOOKS.COM

Edited by Daniel David Moses.
Cover and book design by Duncan Campbell.
Cover image, "Hawk in Flight," by Barnaby Hall / Photonica.
Printed and bound in Canada at Gauvin Press.

Library and Archives Canada Cataloguing in Publication

Lundy, Randy, 1967-
The gift of the hawk / Randy Lundy.

Poems.
ISBN 1-55050-303-0

I. Title.

PS8573.U54398G43 2004   C811'.54   C2004-904996-8

1 2 3 4 5 6 7 8 9 10

COTEAU BOOKS

Available in Canada and the US from:
Fitzhenry & Whiteside

401-2206 Dewdney Ave.   195 Allstate Parkway
Regina, Saskatchewan   Markham, Ontario
Canada   S4R 1H3   Canada   L3R 4T8

The publisher gratefully acknowledges the financial assistance of the Saskatchewan Arts Board, the Canada Council for the Arts, the Government of Canada through the Book Publishing Industry Development Program (BPIDP), the Government of Saskatchewan, through the Cultural Industries Development Fund, and the City of Regina Arts Commission, for its publishing program.

Canada Council
for the Arts
Conseil des Arts
du Canada

SASKATCHEWAN
ARTS BOARD

Canadä

CITY OF REGINA
Regina Arts Commission

This one's for my dad

*and for her—she knows her own name
and needs no man to say it.*

CONTENTS:

The land is what's left
after the failure
of every kind of metaphor.

—PAT LOWTHER,
"COAST RANGE"

Stones are old money with which we rent the world
forgetting that the landscape borrows us
for its own time and its own reason.

—GWENDOLYN MacEWEN,
"STONES AND ANGELS"

BECAUSE YOU ARE BEAUTIFUL I WILL
HAVE *to* TELL YOU *a* NUMBER *of* MY SECRETS.

I am made of stone, not only my heart,
but also my feet and eyes, fire born,
cooled and smoothed, articulated
by a river-tongue.

And though my legs and arms appear
to be limbs, they are roots, travelling in the earth
like moles or lightning,
silent and blind.

My hair is brome or spear grass,
something wild that grows
where others turn to dust, drown
in wind and thirst.

Finally, though I am made of stone,
my heart breathes, flowers, a cactus
holding its own water
and burning.

GIFT *of the* HAWK—1

RITUAL

(for j.s.m.)

Leaves are falling the way blood falls inside her body
when the woman stands to go because
she can no longer remain a girl in her mother's home.

In this season, she gathers what she needs to go on:
plants from the hills, small blue stones, and fragments of petrified
bone from the lakeshore.

And the bones do not care that she has no names
for the animals they once were.

When the moon rises pale as snow, she will hold the bones in her har
and her hands will be as naked as the songs the trees sing. She will bu
sage and juniper, and finally, she will sleep and dream.

She will call out a name and the animal will come.

She will ride upon its back and its face will be her own.

It is the garden you enter in sleep,
to spill the secrets of dreams,
falling like gathered treasures
from the pockets of a child

who is now a woman—

the small stones of the sky
from that river high in the mountains
the feathers of that unidentified bird
from the peregrine's kill-site
and the crow's foot, an inarticulate tongue—

you don't know what to do with it
or what it wants from you—

you've searched so long for someone
who will accept the clawed foot
for the relic it is.

This is the garden whose entrance is hidden
in an undiscovered corner of the yard
behind your childhood home—

where his hands moved
slow and deliberate and white
as the belly of a snake.

It is the garden where you will discover love,
like the inability to forgive, comes
like a thief in the night.

PHOTOGRAPH: AGE 4

(Ipperwash)

I

Your eyes, the same as in that photo
from your childhood

though the girl's small body has grown
into your small woman's body;

sometimes in sleep
they roll back into memory

swim like sunlight on stone
reflected off a slow-flowing river

then, my hands holding your body
are his, scale-shed
                    on your skin.

II

But sometimes your eyes unfold, not fists, but flowers
and they speak, saying

—lobelia, cyclamen, viburnum
                lavender, primrose, portulaca
                        amaryllis, hibiscus, clematis—

a man could devote his life to learning

each sound
each syllable   a petal so fragile

        he breaks and breaks again
                under the weight
                        of their falling.

THE LOST ART *of* WINKING
(at a poetry reading)

Sometimes people look at each other
and their eyes are the soft, wet noses of dogs
sniff-sniffing each other's behinds,
tails carried high in delight.

The first time I saw you, I sniffed you,
nuzzled you till you were damp
and your body felt
the warm breath of my looking.

Your look back was no wet nose.
One eye closed and slowly opened,
the lid gliding across your night-dark eye
and me, like a tongue.

On padded feet, our old cat enters the room
as quietly as moonlight, or the evening breeze,
stretches out on our bed where you sleep;

your breathing sings her into dreams—

she is a thirsting animal travelling
from other rooms, other lives, other times—

over mountains, through valleys,
and across bloomless deserts,
she has journeyed—

the rise and fall of your breathing is a spring
where she has arrived, finally, to drink.

Love descended upon me,
a sickness, a disease that insisted
it would never leave; it descended upon me,
a fever, a plague upon a delirious city;

I have languished
without hope of survival, with no desire
to remain alive.

Now the fever is broken,
and I rise with clear eyes

—but I find love

a steady rain falling
over a drought-dry plain, every morning
some new plant is in bloom—

the prickly pear spreads its blossom
a translucent, earth-bound moon—

and standing, I spread my hands
to gather the medicine that will heal.

Tonight I want your ears, flavour of pumpkin, scent of sage
small peninsulas jutting from a tide of hair.

Tonight I want your toes, released from night, muskeg scent
of wool socks, wild feet dancing in sweet grass and brome.

Tonight I want your breasts, sun-warmed, polished stone
the light of two small moons pressed into my palms.

Tonight I know your body, a pine-shadow eclipse of mine
the glow of cedar smouldering in darkness.

I

The way
a mouth holds
all the unsung
songs of earth
and moon
its pull on tides
its voice hidden
in shells
the way a tongue
enters the silence
curves and shapes
darkness into words
and sings.

II

The way
a flame curves
and holds
a slender stem
of green wood
its tongue draws
a rush of sap
licks and tastes
root and leaf
until wood
snaps and cracks
surrenders at last
entering the silence
of ash.

Take away the corn, the sun-filled fruit of the fields, and all the roots, the water that they hold. Take away the hoofed animals that have given, reluctantly, their flesh. Take away air, sun, the moon and stars. Take them all away.

I depart into the dark, tangled forest of your hair and make a home there. I dwell alone in that night, live as an ascetic, one seeking his vision in the body of the crow, in the eye of the owl. But I come out again, travel past the two new moons of your eyes, and along the gentle ridge of your nose. I pause at, but pass, the dreadful chasm of your lips, and I fall off the edge of the known world as I traverse the incline of your chin down to the hollows of your neck, where willows grow and deer have come to graze. I travel the valley between your breasts, never reaching those peaks, capped by the fading light of day. Onto the plains of your belly my wanderings go, and I pitch a tent there, to study how the cacti grow, to await the sandstorms that blow from the peaks farther north. Deaf and blind, I remember what I know.

One day, I take the long journey to the south, find the sinuous rivers of your thighs, the hummocks of your knees, and the thin passages of your shins. Climbing, at last, the incline of your feet, I discover the many paths of your toes, and, beyond them, the thundering seas.

Here in your eyes is the meadow where the moon, that sky-bone, lies down in the night to sleep with the deer, as round and white as their bellies and breathing as softly, clouds of warm breath rising into the clear autumn air.

Here are the old trees whose leaves the wind cups for a moment in its hand, in its quiet, hollow palm, like hundreds of small minnows in a still and shallow pond, before releasing them like the close and startled flight of birds disturbed by a sigh or a moan, some hidden sound now drowned in the climbing rush of their wings.

Here is the melody of moon and wind, an elemental song sung in the blue drum of the sky, in the green lungs of the grass and leaves, in the red flash of the blackbird's wing, and in the dun-coloured, muscled thigh of the deer as it disappears from the periphery of vision.

AN EXPLANATION

It is the spring scent of the lilac, of roots and earth and lightning, the scent of rain on stone and the nectar bees gather from the wild flowering in the hollows on the wide bellies of the plains, or in the meadows that interrupt the sighing of the pine forests where the deer have come to graze, or in the passes between the volcanic mountain peaks. It is the scent of the evening or morning dew gathered on the tips of your fingers, in the inlets between your toes. It is the scent of these earthy things that brings this singer with nothing but his small drum of a voice.

It is nothing but these scents that bring this wandering mendicant here to wait, as one might wait by the side of a track for a train to come in the night. It is nothing but these scents that bring him here to spend his time worshipping, beneath moon and stars, the flesh that releases such pleasure into the darkness, happy to leave a song of his own here in the palms of your hands, in the curve of your thighs, in the arch of your spine, until the season when the corn is harvested and the vines are growing black.

I

In darkness, fingers slide over skin
searching for what is missing, an emptiness
the telltale tissue of a scar—

two thumbs, twenty-four ribs
a careful inventory, no absence
I can detect by touch.

Yet, when I reach out beyond my self
there you are   still
                              sleeping beside me.

II

Beneath their lids
your eyes roll like lazy fish
koi in the emperor's garden.
Somewhere your spirit sits on a low bench
beneath cedar, cypress, and pine
seeking the serenity of water
falling over stone. Your eyes open
like the blossom on the dwarf rose
that sits on our mantel. Slowly.
Your eyes open slowly to the light.

III

Perhaps the emptiness I seek
is not to be found
in the cage of my ribs
my searching in the night

or in the emptiness a mind is
before the spirit returns to the body
or in the emptiness light is
before the eye begins to see

—perhaps there is only
the emptiness of your womb
when the moon is full
and like a tide I am pulled
into the deep silence of the sea.

It was that other one, that damned
silly husband of hers. See,
he didn't know the joke.

You know the one—
red on the outside,
white on the inside.

She saw the buds on the trees
watching her with thin green eyes.
Her, she just winked at them and danced.

Later, they became friends, her and the leaves.
When they laughed, she laughed, their voices
rising from inside the same deep belly.

Meanwhile, her husband, he was always busy
whispering with that bearded one,
whispering and looking at her, giggling
like a coupla hormonal schoolboys.

Her, she would just wink and dance
flash a bit of thigh or breast.

See her, she talked with all the animals.

Sometimes even with that one,
that long, skinny, twisting one,
the one with the eyes like the budding leaves.
He was all slurs and spit that one.

But sometimes, she would wrap him
around her dancing body
and teach him to use his tongue properly.

One day her husband, that damned
silly one, he bites the apple
and then they have to leave.

Her, she didn't eat no apple.
Cuz see, she knows, she knows
you are what you eat.

That time the blackbirds lifted from the branches
leaves falling in reverse, rising into the late dusk
of the river valley.

I pulled you close, reached out, like night
reaching out to embrace the birds.

The branches of the aspen then, trembling, empty
the buds breathing a first breath, ready to accept
flight or rest, ready to hold
these small dark bodies.

They circled three times before settling again.

Later, your breath was like a first breathing
a rising and falling, a sound like sudden flight—

your eyes fluttering, finally closing
a folding of wings.

EARLY SPRING: DREAMING *a* GARDEN

That night you dreamed of the garden
you would plant in the spring
how you would work the ground
turn it back upon itself
until it warmed and breathed.

Your mind filling with blossoms
sunflowers and wild lilies
flares of colour, slender tendrils
wisteria and sweet peas
climbing toward the light.

The next morning, standing at your window
I saw a magpie laughing in the branches of an elm
breaking dried twigs for a nest, behind this
the moon, bone-pale owl-stone, a cratered face
carved by starlight, a sign whose meaning
I could not speak.

Tonight, I am far away and remembering.

Invisible in the distance, geese call
and turn northward, a coyote barks its hunger
into the hills, bare with stories and song.

In the morning, I too will begin a return
through a valley filled with fog.

When I arrive, I will tell you
of these signs I cannot read
how I long to be the earth, holding
the long sleep of seeds.

PRAYER *to* NINE DEER
(south of Humboldt, SK)

Nine whitetails on the edge of the field
hold us in rapt attention, our stillness a mirror of theirs—

one, a doe, turns, ambles over the edge of the bluff,
out of sight, appears on the crest of the next rise—

a fawn pauses to look back
across the growing distance between us—

how casually they leave.

My prayer to this moment, these deer—
that your eyes will never retreat

drifting away into the hills
shifting without effort into the night.

Do you remember those islands
where we gathered driftwood, shells,
and memories of our separate pasts?

Like the humped backs of whales
travelling upriver in the night
they have slipped beneath the surface.

But listen, you can still hear their songs
those moans and sighs rising,
singing from the river's bed.

Slowly you begin to emerge
from sleep, and there is a moment
when sleep and waking converge—

in the dream, you were with someone,
a lover, a face and voice—

you can almost hear her
chanting your name—

receding now, further away
than any memory—

just before you awake,
you are in a garden, but alone.

Birds are singing. Suddenly your eyes
are blinking in the too bright light.

The birds have become real,
serrated feathers and glinting beaks.

And birdsong encroaches, drawing you into the day
the only singing you can hear.

No-moon night.
She seems to be coming around
more often lately.
This absence.

In our low-lying bed
your body, curled and white
eclipsed by the heaviness
of the goosedown blanket.

Beside you
a different kind of weight—

the still-warm depression
of my sleeplessness.

CRANBERRY FLATS

(for Buryl)

All afternoon, we roam the banks of the river, collecting shells coloured like the northern lights. We collect the wind-hollowed bones of birds, birds whose songs once disturbed the sleep of stones with visions of migratory flight. We gather lumps of coal, plants surrendered to a deep mineral sleep. These and the blue-bleached claws of crayfish, each clenched around its small emptiness.

In a month, our breathing, like the slow turning of leaves as they fall, will settle upon the river, and sink into its flow.

MIGRATIONS
(St. Peter's Abbey)

In this season, the sun meditates
naked, shivering low on the horizon.

She is a nun with empty palms
someone who has let go of everything.

She lives back in the trees where the bare
branches creak, the song of the ascetic.

She keeps company with the crows
whose silence will be the invocation of cold.

She sees their eyes are new moons
their feathers an eclipse of the weakening light.

If she dreams of death and loss, its cause is
the absence of these birds.

MEMORY
(Eastend, SK)

Night is a raven, moon
a bright stone in its beak, broad wings
stir a breeze beneath the eaves
of the house where I sleep
far from everything I know—

stars drag their noisy, old light
over the roof, claws clicking
across shingles—

in the hills, some animal is singing
a song for the end of things.

In the morning, I too will find words
like feathers caught in the trees—

I will find names to hold
all of the things I fear—

but now a leaf browns and curls
around its last breath—I sleep
and dream—

you have fallen away from me—

as far away as a story I tell
in words I no longer believe.

FABULIST

Once again, fabulist, you have fooled
only yourself. The wind's noise may be without plot,
but its peregrinations have torn a hole
in the night, where your heart hunches
like a new moon—a random possibility
without light.

Fabulist, you have fooled yourself—
trying to tear a song from the long
gullet of the worm, trying to tug a song
from the sleeping throat of the bird.

You thought a song might save you
but found only a few tuneless words
and tonight, the darkness of the sky is deep.

Your only hope is to fly
sightless and blind like a bat.
You must get down on your knees
and perform one silent, perfect act.

Once you spoke with trees
with river and fish, with stones and sun.
Now when you chant your prayer, an incantation
sung into the completeness of this night,
you hear only a faint echo, your own voice
and the slow pulsing of the stars.

The spider's web snares sun's first light, splays a spectrum
through night's last dew. And the light does not struggle

and drops of dew are not tears. Like so much beauty
it begins with hunger. This woven labyrinth

of beginnings and endings. What are you searching for
the centre or a way out? You must decide—

your wings are vibrating in fear
and the many-eyed spinner is near.

All night the river tangles and untangles
weaves and unweaves, braids and unbraids

—a long mane flowing in the wind
a necessity it alone can feel—

churning, stirring sediment, lumps of coal
shards of bone, empty shells.

All night, your mind, glowing fragment of stone
drifts upon the waters, moon-horse running toward the horizon

—instinct leading the animal toward dawn
somewhere beyond seeing.

When dawn finally comes, it finds your body
turning in an uneasy sleep, your face a sunflower facing the rising sun

—everything you have become, like the night
unravelling in first light.

—a tiny fossil
from a prehistoric sea
locked forever
in my quiet heart—

cold stone.

Your words find me
like a knife finds the spine

of a fish　　　　　　　gasping

pulled from a winter hole
its wide eye　　　　filled with afternoon moon

its mouth struggling
with an element it will never learn.

Your words　　　　blood on snow
find me like a blade

a serrated separation　　　flesh from bone.

That woman you loved. She told you
she knew you would leave her. Your hands
feather-spread upon her body. Casting a winged
shadow on her skin. A hawk's wings pinning its prey.

She told you she could feel it in her bones. The first time.
She could hear their crack. As she trembled. A sound
like river ice in the growing spring light. A sudden knowing.
A flow of dark water singing beneath our feet.

Remember. The first time you knew. Sitting on the front step.
The concrete warmed by early-October sun. The wind
fleeing through dried stalks of corn. Two crows hunched
in an elm, too tired to say anything, too tired to tell a story
that would make any of this make any sense.

The lines of retreating
geese flee
the perfect silence and cold
of the season to come—

they are sutures, each body
a single stitch, black
as the frost-touched vine
rotting in the garden, each belly
the raised whiteness
of deadened flesh—

and all of this
unable to close
the wounds their voices are—

wounds that open and close
like flowers—

in a single breath.

Tonight, the sky
so covered with scars
I wonder
what has seeped in or out
what has been infected
or emptied—

I wonder what stories
we will tell ourselves—

to survive
this season of descent.

At first light, a single crow tests its voice
against the current of cold in the wind.

Moon's eye is blackened, earth-shadow
the imprint of jealous knuckles.

Earth, tilted on its axis, wobbles through space
circling the block, not quite sure where it's going.

Crow has an idea, but at this early hour
who's listening to his shouts?

Sometimes when I hold you
my body is the fist of a young boy—

he spends the afternoon
at the far edge of the field
where he discovers a nest
of small pink bodies
and he thinks—

there are six of them, no
the mother will not miss one—

he is running
across dark-turned furrows
he needs someone
to share his secret—

reaching the back steps of the house
he stops when he realizes
the small body in his palm
is no longer moving
and the cat is winding
around his ankles—

he opens his hand
and the dead thing
falls into the dust.

Much later, he will dream of this day
but he will see it all from a distance—

an eight-year-old boy runs
across a freshly turned field—

the sun and the heat, his small, booted feet
kicking up a trail of dust behind him
excitement and fear on his face—

the cat feasts and as he kneels
she caresses his soft palm into a fist
with her sharp tongue—

he dreams and remembers
the cat and her tongue and how
he kicked her again and again.

In the Bikini Bar in the city
the mostly naked waitress
serves beer for minimum wage
plus tips.

And tonight, you're not tipping
like you're from a small town.

She walks away, the sway of her hips
guiding your eyes into a slide down
the thin, inward curve of her spine
a slight water-carved-in-stone indentation.

And, you're not thinking of your wife
sleeping five hundred miles away.

You're imagining your tongue
a slender rivulet of water
following the lay of the land
seeking out those low spots
seeking out the muskeg scent
of wet moss and pine.

First of all, the word soul
it just will not do
with its implication
its insinuation
its outright declaration
that the body is a tomb!

Any body
who has properly lived as such
will know this is true.

Makes me think of a friend
who went home with a woman
was led into a dark room
with chain-mail curtains
suspended from the ceiling
only to discover a coffin
would be the stage
for the opening of her womb.

Well, he wasn't about
to screw in a coffin
although I'd like to think he did
that I would
and that you would too.

In life, death
was a thing you dreamed of

—as you slept on my chest, I watched
your eyes moving beneath their lids, following
the paths of mice or the flight of birds.

Having lived your entire life
indoors, this dreaming of death
was only a dreaming, an imagining
of a life unlived, yet it was something
alive inside of you. Your starts and growls
the unsheathing of your claws, betraying
the secrets of your sleep.

Death lived in you then, and so, perhaps
there is now some remainder of life
in your death.

In the days to come, I will brush your fur
from my clothes, pick the shed sheaths of claws
from the bed where I sleep and dream.

When these are gone, I will still have
the whiskers I have gathered and kept
in a wooden box on the mantel—

those fragile reminders of how we measure
the small spaces of our lives.

You held a bowl to his mouth, hoping
he would drink, hoping that this day
of all the long, hot days of that August
would be different.

But the dog lay in the shade
refusing to drink or eat, the saliva
gathering and thickening on his lips
like maggots on rotting flesh.

Then came the heaviness, the leaning
of all your young weight on the shovel,
the glint of the blade, the smell
of the turned soil.

A few inches below the surface
the topsoil gave way to gravel
and you bruised your hands
against the burying. They would throb
for four days, a memory your body
would bring back in old age, when
your bones began to ache.

There was a moment in this
when you forgot whether you were digging
a grave or turning the earth in search
of something buried but forgotten.

Then it passed, and you remembered
you were here to lay something to rest.

Only later would you come to understand
how memories are made.

THE WASP

When the wasp tries to enter the window
wave your hands wildly
because you know it will enter the house
and in its persistence and desperation
try to make a home there
and you will have to kill it
because a man cannot live the winter
with wasps.

And it makes no sense
but you are thinking of that woman
at the party on Saturday
how she was drunk and angry
confused and looking for her husband
wanting to bite him again and again
with the sharp teeth of her pain
how you stumbled away from her
waving your hands to ward her off
and how your hands have felt
heavy since that night.

Something in you afraid of something in her
so like a wasp in search of an opening
into a warm place.

HOPE

I am thinking of the spider
the rack of its delicate body.
How it is mostly abdomen, mostly gut.

How it stretches a web
across the emptiness
between the brittle reach of twigs.

Or across the emptiness
at the convergence of walls and ceiling
in a breathless, dry-moth room.

How the convergence is a kind of completion.
Matter supporting matter. A shelter for the mind.
A home.

The peering moon is the spider's only witness
and again she has nothing to say, a frost-touched bud
wrapped up in her own peculiar darkness.

But I am thinking of the spider.

How it drags from its body
thin filaments of hope, suspended

—a shimmering geometry of death
extended from inside
a moon-dark gut.

small fish
flash in moonlight—

fireflies
among reeds—

a great blue heron
motionless—

a patience
perfected by need—

Trying to find the words to describe
the beauty of the dragonfly caught in the spider's web,
its four wings kaleidoscoping afternoon light.

And the beauty of struggle, the spider's bite, the slowing
of the wingbeat, the curling of the slender blue body,
the shape of wind in a wave on the lake.

And the slow, deliberate spinning of the shroud,
the spider dragging its prize.

Trying to find the words to describe to you
how we drag behind us all of the deaths
our innocent hungers
have caused.

Mid-afternoon and the moon is out
—a sun-bleached bird's skull in the sand—
and the crows speaking of this solitude and that

but they are never alone, these wraiths
falling from the pines, their voices and bodies
an absence of two, or three, or ten

punctuating the silence, the light
leading the reluctant mind, the widening eye
to that place where some small thing has died.

FOR ALL *of* THOSE WHO HAVE DIED *at the* HANDS *of* MEN
(for Shelley Napope, Eva Taysup, & Calinda Waterhen)

I too have cradled death in my hands, its stone-weight heavy as tonight's moon, full and low, so close I could touch it if I wasn't so afraid. These hands. Palms up, fingers curled, like the dried spider in this room's far corner. I still carry the deaths I have caused with my tools, emptiness and rage, a craftsman working through nights and days.

I stopped hunting because of that gut-shot squirrel, dragging its intestines behind it as it ran along a branch, until it fell, suspended there, its four small hands grasping at the emptiness the sky was that day, a small torn and tangled offering left for the crows.

I think of the rabbit's crying like a child until I brought my boot down in mercy or to save myself from the sound. Who can say why men kill, what it takes to stop the trembling storm inside? All I know is that nothing I have ever made has replaced the beauty I have destroyed.

Climbing down
long braids of smoke
these old ones
their voices
dried leaves
crunching underfoot—

marrow turned to dust
in the jaws of a starving animal.

They're summoned
by the sour scent
of soup, the sweet aroma
of prairie fruit, to wet
their withered lips—

throats closed like a fist
around a weathered song.

Night, magpie wing-tip blue
embracing moon's full light.

Behind a heavy robe of cloud
aurora borealis dances.

In this car, two of us travelling
in silence toward the past.

In our basket of steel and glass
we might be the First Ones—

in their basket of woven willow
a basket of rib-cage bone

the hole we leave behind us
the thread that leads us home.

OLD WOMAN

In that interval between
sleep   and   waking
you are the dream

ancient and fragile
thin as the dragonfly's wing
its humming song
lifted on wind
old as stone

your toes
dancing fireflies
yellowed claws
tracing arcs in the air

your face
wrapped in gauze
feline eyes
whiskers sprouting
from your chin.

You are the cricket
perched in our ears
chanting prophecies
we forget by day

—singing—

O dead dead
A stinking old bundle of
                                    dead.

The man left the farm when he was young
maybe sixteen, to work in a logging camp.
With his first paycheque, he bought his mother,
the one he hit before he left, a set of silverware.
For the next thirty-some-odd years, he worked
far from home, in mines and lumber mills.

Two ex-wives and one son later, he lost his job
and the promise of a pension; it was 1982.

He found part-time work, driving an old farm truck,
picking up garbage in a trailer court, and made friends
with the neighbourhood kids.

Then one day, the man died.

No one noticed, except his son;
who noticed only because there was no money
to pay for the funeral, the embalming,
the wood and brass coffin, and the small plot of ground.

Even if he managed to pay for it
the son would not visit the grave
for ten years, or twenty, or never.

This was the son's inheritance:

a box of socks, new and unworn
found at the back of his father's closet
at the far end of the trailer
that still reeked of the body
undiscovered for three days;

they were polyester, bought on sale
at a discount store in the city;
each time the son wore them
his feet would sweat and then freeze
so that every time his feet got cold and blue
he would think of his father.

That's it.

Oh, except the neighbourhood kids noticed too;
on Monday, they asked the stranger in the red truck
what happened to their garbage man.

Except the son would never know this.

Thank you for coming.

You stood on a long finger of stone
pointing itself into the lake
drawing your attention to the water
rising and falling on the driftwood shores;

your face was smooth
deerhide stretched on a drum
a few bloodstains on the skin
birthmarks on the belly of a son;

your hair, long and fluid
would later become brittle moss
abandoned for the winter
on the southern facing
spines of the trees;

your face would carry
the marks of the land that bore it
a country of rock, sheared
by wind and rain, grooved by ice
a few scars from the hand
of a man who loved you;

in those grooves gathered bits of soil
where seeds settled and began
to sing their green prayers to the sky;

soon bark and leaves
growing from the inside out
memory ringed around itself;

that night my father's hands gripped you
the hands of a miner on the thin wrist of a pick—

the hands of a man
who brought food to you and your children
when your husband was nowhere to be found
raising his whiskey-filled glass to the night, to a friend
to some woman who was not you—

they gripped you
roots gripping the barren stone
the last thing they had to hold onto—

and the stone inside your body fell
like a full, winter moon

and a new season
you had no names for
was born.

I

I imagine her
a young girl filling the feeder
knowing the grosbeaks will come
yellow and black, sunlight and shadow in the leaves;
she feels the breeze brush her cheek
like a wing or a hand.

II

I remember her
a small woman between
the carefully spaced rows of her garden
bent over, studying the progress of potatoes and peas
at the edge of the garden a single row of sunflowers
the sun singing full the seeds.

III

Grandmother, the flax is blooming early
blue as the veins in your hands
and the canola is blooming too
bright as those flowers you planted
to feed the birds that you knew
would not leave.

She is twig-fingered. Cedar-skinned. Sweetgrass-braided hair. She is open-eyed, onyx-eyed dreamer, dwelling deep in the moonless, forested cavern of your skull. She does both what you can and what you cannot do. She is companion of bat, consort of owl. In your hand, she places raven feather, bear scat—and his hand.

That man you had forgotten, had tried to forget.

She leads you to the slow flow of river. She says, *Sit. Sit here. See how it moves. See how it all moves.* You think the dark water is sky. You think it is earth, but *No,* she says. *This is old water, and you must sit here. Be as stone, the two of you, as full and as empty. Be as one stone, moved by water, moved by ice. Rubbed by wind and the heavy-shouldered buffalo. Sit here, on this old lakeshore. What you seek is here. It is here. Deep in the sediment, you will find what you seek. The* moon, she lies buried here like some slow creature of the sea.

I'm praying that you're a bear and that the where you've gone into is only hibernation. Praying that your bones will gather sinew and flesh. I'm praying the way roots search among stones for fallen rain and push green blades into the blue.

Praying that in this way you too will emerge, thin and hungry into the growing light, the memory of berries upon your tongue like a purple bruise, your hunger waking and leading you from this darkness that will have been a womb.

I imagine you standing inside the belly of a great bronze bell.
Its weight suspended around you like a cowl,
the weight of knowing
you are alone. There is no wind.
It is neither day nor night. Standing
in the silence, naked to the waist and waiting.

It is the time for rituals, the time of corn and gourds,
locks of hair, the bones of birds.

Your hand reaches out, strokes the metal,
harder than a man's mind
and body after a lifetime of work.
And there is a singing in the bell.
Do you recognize the voice in your bones?
It is a song without words,
the song a son sings when his father has died.

It is the singing of a father's bones in the earth.
As stones move above him
like slow moons. Aligning for the moment of birth.

In the grave, my father's bones
brittle as starlight just before dawn—

the stars reach out to embrace the night
and break beneath its weight—

just before birds begin to sing
a silence grows and holds—

bones and stars and moon.

There's nothing out here
nothing to interrupt
the mind or the eye
as it wanders
a herd of horses
toward the horizon.

Out here, the earth pulls flat
as your lover's stomach
under the sky hovering
everywhere at once.

The heat of the sun
with its beating wings
in its talons some dead thing
to feed your hunger.

Out here
your mind, your eye
is hungry, naked—

the new cry of a hawk
breaking through its shell.

The silence you must find
is not the near silence
of the deer mouse, a rustling
in a fallow field.

The silence you must find
is like the wing of a red-
tailed hawk, riding a late afternoon
updraft, until it almost touches
the sun.

A silence like that wing—

slicing through air
cleaving sunlight in two
devouring the distance to earth.

But this is not enough.

The silence you seek
is a darkness and a stillness
bestowed by the perfection of talons.

The sky this evening lit
like the belly of a rainbow trout
spawning into darkness.

It is not much
but I want to tell you
this—

the light passing over
until nothing is left
but—

the shadow of a wing—

night and starlight—

           bones picked clean.

The moon rises so full
its light like water

lifted from a spring
overflows

the dark, cupped
hands of the night.

There is a stone you return to. The one
where the crayfish offer their bodies to the light.
It will bleach them blue and leave them there
through the whole night. The patience of this stone.
To sit by the river for years. Saying nothing. With no one
but the stars for company. The patience of this stone.
To accept so much dying.

BEAR

(for Susan G.)

Late-summer sunlight, reflected off the river's slow flow
afternoon aurora on patient river stones;

when the bear emerges onto the bank
to dip its muzzle and drink

stones exhale warm breath into dusk
sigh in wet, clay-heavy sleep;

the animal lifts its heavy head in a broad-nostril flare
its senses leaning to the far-bank stir of leaves;

your breathing   hesitates
while the bear's mouth spills mist, and he snorts

the first stars into the darkening eastern sky.

You knew it would come to this. You are alone
hunched beneath a carapace of sky, stars shining
like stones in slow water. Words haven't abandoned you
but have retreated, dogs scared off by the scent
of something wild. You can hear their yelps and whines
coming from the porch where they pace nervous circles
in the light, their cacophony a tame imitation
of the coyote's song rising from the hills. Out here
trees bend low in wind, and your body is a perfect word
an inarticulate tongue, a new moon fallen among stones
releasing its heavy breath in the night.

It was easy to believe as the century was closing
that the world was ending. But now you know
the millennium has turned and nothing has changed.

At the edge of these hills, red ants biting your legs,
mosquitoes biting you everywhere else. These and
the dragonflies and the damselflies a blue hovering.
The hum of their wings an amber-coloured song.

Since the ranchers have quit grazing their cattle here
juniper, sagebrush, and fescue have insinuated themselves
into the bald dunes. Nothing has ended.

Not even the mice, whose delicate bones you gather
as if they are relics, and perhaps they are. A hawk
has left these offerings, but you don't know
how to respond.

The hawk has fed, his belly distended like the waxing moon;
he has entered sleep and the beetle has left its hieroglyphic trail
and disappeared beneath the surface of the sun-bleached sand.
The hawk has fed

but his hunger has not ended; it has subsided with the wind
its last sigh hanging like the low but rising moon.

The earth is too damp for anything tonight
except birth, the rebirth of that woman's body,
the moon, from moist soil;

all month she has waned thin
brittle, pale as a blade of grass
in a season of drought;

now she is a mushroom
swelling from the forest floor.

You sing an invitation
calling her into the room
your mouth is;

when she arrives her light
will spread itself like a sheet
on the smooth bed of your tongue;

she will bring silence there
like love
and your song will settle
on her cheek
a descending breath or hand
or the wings of a moth;

it will leave a faint trace of dust
what the body holds
after the mind has closed its doors
to wander the insomniac halls
of sleep.

This is the darkness she enters
behind teeth, at the opening of the throat;

this is the darkness that begins
the dream of a body
made of nothing
but pure light and
stone.

A Few Notes:

The title of the first poem in the book is a line from Gwendolyn MacEwen's poem "Afterworlds," and the title "The Garden of Thieves" is borrowed from a MacEwen poem. Each can be found in *Afterworlds*.

The title "The river's reclaimed the islands I loved" is a line from Anne Hebert's poem "A Minor Despair" found in *Selected Poems*, trans. A. Poulin, Jr.

"On the Death of a Cat" borrows its title from a Franz Wright poem published in the December 15, 2003 edition of the *New Yorker*.

"The Night of My Conception" is a title borrowed from a Patrick Lane poem found in *The Bare Plum of Winter Rain*.

The italicized lines that conclude "Old Woman" are from Anne Szumigalski's poem "Nettles" found in *Dogstones: Selected and New Poems*.

The italicized lines that begin the poem "Praying" are from Daniel David Moses's poem "A Prayer and Her Hands Folded in a Bedside Manner" found in *Sixteen Jesuses*.

The italicized lines in "The Sound" are borrowed (with altered line breaks) from Patrick Lane's poem "We have begun to bury ourselves" found in *no longer two people*, by Patrick Lane and Lorna Uher.

A Few Thank Yous:

To Damon, Buryl, Francie, Diane, and Jill, for their friendship; to the Thai family, for a home away from home; and to the Sunday brunch crew. To Gail and Bernie, for being better colleagues than I often deserve. To all of the students I have met in classes over the years, especially to the students in the 2004 edition of English 352, for making me a better editor and for stretching my understanding of what a poem can be and do. To Daniel David Moses, for his care in reading and hearing these poems.

DATE DUE	RETURNED

About

Randy ...a
memb ...
wester ...
Saskat ...
in Sas ...
currer ...

Randy ...
publis ...is
his se ...es
such a ...
Native Poetry in Canada: A Contemporary Anthology, and
Without Reservation: Indigenous Erotica. He has worked
for the First Nations University of Canada (formerly the
Saskatchewan Indian Federated College), in Saskatoon
and Regina, as a tutor, a lecturer, and a writer-in-
residence. He is currently an Assistant Professor of
English in the First Nations University's Department of
English.